Judith K. Witherow

ALL THINGS WILD

Poems *from the* Appalachians

Judith K. Witherow

Thank you, Cheryl, without your help I'd still be struggling with this! SUE

Twin Spirits Publishing

'Not just another pretty DBA'

Twin Spirits Publishing
Post Office Box 1237
Clinton, Maryland 20735

Licensed use photograph - page 26. All other photographs and cover art by Sue Lenaerts and Judith K. Witherow.

Library of Congress Control Number: 2003115929

ISBN 0-9747172-0-7

Dedicated to my mother
Almeda
and my forever partner
Sue.
They instilled in me the love
and wisdom of poetry.
Words are not just letters
grouped together in a book.
A book is more than a
weight to keep your
mind propped open.

ACKNOWLEDGEMENTS

Some of the poetry in this book first appeared in the following:

AMERICAN POETRY ANTHOLOGY: Quietus
DREAMS: Pity The Poet
EAGLE WING PRESS: Nature In Balance
EXPRESSIONS: The First Frost
HEY: Haiku, Who Knew?
MY LOVER IS A WOMAN: Here In The Forest
NEW POETS/ONE: Sioux
QUILL AND PARCHMENT: Contemplating Chaos, Play It My Way, Sweet Flowing Memories, My Promise, (Haiku - first born birds of spring, mother's day roses, squirrels at feeder, the pinto pony)
SPARROWGRASS: Leaves
STARFISH: (Haiku - the pinto pony)
WAYAH REVIEW: Sister Sioux, Here In The Forest, Quietus, Nature In Balance

INTRODUCTION

All Things Wild was inspired by everyone and everything that was ever typecast as untamed and untrained. In civilization, "wild" and "wildness" are words that are used when a class definition can't be found to categorize that which is not easily understood. Poetry and poverty are two examples of words that many place in this realm. In my life they have always been woven tighter than wisteria vines.

Nature catalogs her own descriptions, but many humans refuse to accept what those of us close to the earth deem as fact of the highest spiritual truth. "Fact" and "fiction" are merely words used to confound and control those who walk outside the borders of belief.

Whenever you fail to become breathless at the sight of a sky full of clouds playing tag with the wind you have lost that wildness. Should you come upon a garden of cat o' nine tails or a field of milkweed pods bursting with seed, and keep walking, you are lost to the wilderness of windows and doors.

If the sight of someone you have loved for decades still leaves you filled with want-to and wonder you have remained untamed and untrained. Society decrees that time diminishes wildness and wild into a settled routine. Being apart for a day shouldn't have you mentally pacing like a caged animal unless you thrive in the world of totems and omens.

All things wild should never be put inside anything that might constrain movement or reason for being. If a definition is needed to explain the inexplicable then you have become too close to "reality." To unlock this mystery you have to willingly lose yourself in the words written by one who is on intimate terms with the Spirit world.

Judith K. Witherow

CONTENTS

NATURE IN BALANCE

When birds of prey
do earthward glide,
to search the meadows
where unwary reside.
Swift is their sighting,
no breaking of stride.
Curved talons at ready,
shrill screeches of pride.
Fulfilling the ritual
that faint hearts deride,
Nature's the choreographer
when two worlds collide.

QUIETUS

The mountains were
awaiting me,
just as I believed
they would.
Neither condemning nor
approving,
knowing that surface
is surface.
Waiting for the unveiling
of underneath,
for feelings long forgot
to spill out.
An echo to careen across
the mountains,
repeated in unremitting
certainty.
I'm home, I'm home
for good;
what humans forsake
nature reclaims.

cat o' nine tails burst
coloring the ground with white
snowshoes are useless

mushroom umbrellas
tip their caps to everyone
dancing in the rain

LEAVES

They don't change much,
except maybe a little
showing of bud or three
in the birthing of Spring.

Then again, there's Summer.
It finds them turning every
which-a-way shade of green,
all decked out and dancing.

And Fall! Fall discovers
each and every one coated
and colored in eager arrival
of an early frost or freeze.

Just when you think you can't
absorb one more droplet of
beauty, they up and weep their
leaves in deference to Winter.

CONTEMPLATING CHAOS

In the quiet
of the riot,
when the reason
trickles in.

When the heat
of hatred passes,
and the surge of
violence ends.

As the smoke
and ashes settle,
blotting out
the noonday sun.

Will we stop
to seek the answers,
or continue
once again?

THE FIRST FROST

Hold back,
        Hold back I say.

Be slow to trample
over gardens
green and yielding
awesome bounty
        without ceasing.

Cloak still in warmth
the fragrant rose
and mighty sunflower
bent ground-low with
        swollen seed.

And cast no shadow
on the leaf
that when removed
will crazy-quilt
        its summer sheen.

Nor toe dance across
the mountaintop
swirling and whirling
leaving winter
        in your wake.

Hold back,
        Hold back I say.

Author's former Appalachian home (right)

POVERTY ISN'T PRETTY

The windows framed
by tattered plastic curtains
allow the sun to sift through
yellowed paper shades.
Shadows circle and surround
the nearly full slop bucket.
Houseflies land and take
flight without ceasing.
To them it doesn't matter
if you're awake or asleep.
The fear of being swatted
long ago lost meaning.
What I loved most
about the daylight,
besides the warmth,
was the way it always
kept the rats at bay.

APPALACHIANS

With my nose pressed flat
to the soot smudged window
I gaze out at the mountains.
Nodding in satisfaction
that they're right where
I'd left them at nightfall.
Consistency. That's what
life's all about.
The water bucket might
be frozen to the trough.
All the chunks of coal
and slab wood will burn
faster than expected.
The food reserve might
hold out and feed all
skinny eight of us.
Yeah, smudged windows
sure can taunt the truth.
Damn the rain. It pours
through more roof holes
than there are pans and
cans to catch it in.
Still, these mountains
remain constant. They soothe
and salve better then any
home grown or store got
medicine I've yet to find.

purple fleshy figs
swaying in the summer breeze
ooze their pulp and seed

come little leaves
drench me in autumn colors
chase away the blues

icicles growing
wind and cold protect their length
until droplets form

nubile birds of spring
preen their unruly feathers
in search of a mate

RHYTHM AND HUES

Where have all the
sun-brushed women gone?
Gone to cover each and
every one.
Can't hide their faces,
won't dye their hair.
Different drums
signal each foot
to tap and stamp.
Bodies sway; heads nod
with the heartbeat of
knowledge.
Call it rhythm.
Say it's the blues.
Pound on stretched hides
and whisper it's old name,
Indian chicken scratch.
Music will always be the
caress and the carrion
of life.
The dance of destiny
always needs a partner,
and she who knows the steps
is the choice of
the Spirits.

SIOUX

I will walk softly over your
soul
with moccasined feet,
taking care never to trample
your dreams.
Knowing that life has not
always
been kind,
I will leave nothing but the
imprints
of love.

SOUNDS LIKE LOVE

The way you talk
that singing sound
causes each bird to
tilt their tiny head
as if listening for
a favorite food.
What is that sound
that brings everything
in nature to a halt?
It's you who walks
the earth with
clouds cuddled ‘round
your slim shoulders.
Crows feet dance upon
the corners of
your eyes as laughter
rolls along the ridgetop.

PLAY IT MY WAY

Woe, Lord,
here comes that
searing, soaking
sadness again.
Great puddles
of teardrops do
the Texas two-step
out the door
and cascade down
the salt pocked
sidewalk.
Someone bring me
ALL those Al Green,
Sainte-Marie and
Etta James CD's.
I need walking,
wailing, sitting,
sobbing ballads
to match my mood.
Nothing lite could
possibly ease or
set me free.
These Shamans help
me ponder living,
dying, or merely
wanting to survive
your leaving.

HERE IN THE FOREST

Lie down with me
on a blanket
of long needled pine.
Let me cover you
with multi-colored leaves.
The moon and stars
will dim their light
to shield us.
Here in the darkness
skin color
goes unnoticed.
Here in the forest
my Native ways
are natural.

awash in moonlight
female wolf mournfully howls
echoes blend and bleed

OUT OF BODY

I was many a mile
down the twisty road
before you took notice
of my leaving.

You never believed
in omens and tellings.
Your habitat was all
textbook and territory.
Don't bother checking,
there's no make-up
course.

Once upon a time I
floated overhead
while you tried to detour
the better part of me.

SWEET FLOWING MEMORIES

The oft played tune
of "Misty Blue,"
slow dancing taught
when love was new.

A camping trip
to Ocean City.
Stroh Lites sipped
and talk was witty.

Dorthy Moore,
oh so soulful,
spilled her magic
and made us whole.

Memories, they
drench my being,
with joyous thoughts
that we've created.

There truly is
one absolute,
a love like ours
time won't dilute.

THE ICARUS COMPLEX

Glows hot the orb
that beckons freely,
yet shields its heat
so moths will follow.

Into that void
I soared with purpose,
on feathered wings
that wax held firmly.
Those haughty skies
did tempt ascension,
with no regard
to earth-held limits.

"Just see the light,"
it thundered grandly.
"Come view the world
as you perceive it."

Propelled to heights
mere fools just dream of,
where wind-sucked laughs
did meld and blend,
I conquered all,
no world restrained me,
till gravity wrenched
loose its pull.

DREAM WEAVER

The dreams they
keep on coming,
dreams of death
dreams of illness.

The animals keep
showing me,
scenes of sadness
signs of sickness.

Big racked moose
charge with
hooves that slice
the air in madness.

Skunks with mouths
that foam and menace,
gnawing at my body
stiff and lifeless.

The night no longer
dares to shield me.
It lies in wait to
catch me napping.

Grandfather chants
while teardrops run,
rocking to and fro
with both feet tapping.

The neighbor's dogs
continue howling
late into the night.
Death is on the prowl.

Even if these Spirits
fail to discover me,
I won't go undetected.
They'll continue stalking.

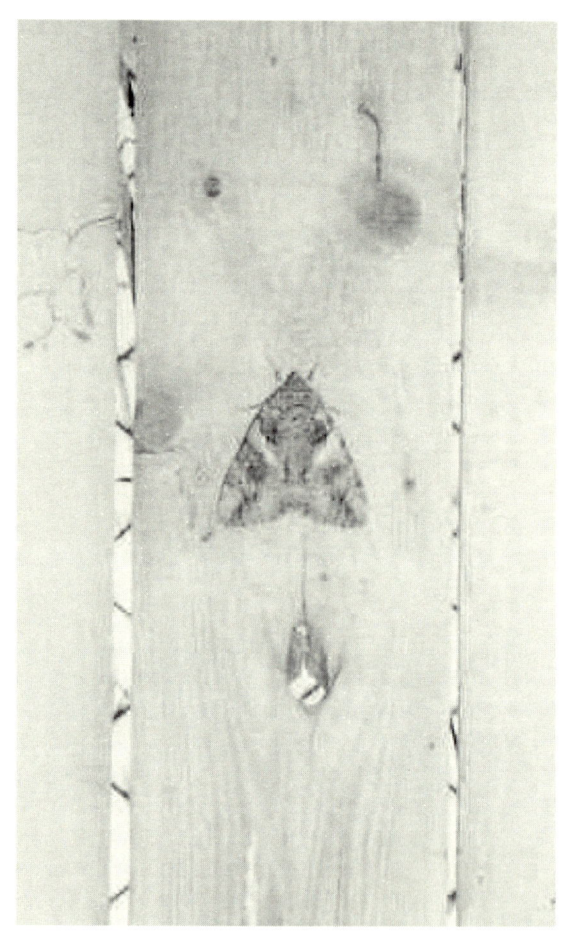

grey moth circles flame
each orbit brings her closer
to the end of flight

PITY THE POET

Just one of those drift
days
Where the tongue is one
beat
Behind the brain.

Commonplace things and
people
Are blurred by spider web
shrouds.
Pity the poet.

YOUR STATISTICS

Don't ask me how many
eagle nests I spotted
on my walk along the
litter pocked shore.

Count and catalog
them on your own.

Nor will I speak of
the old beaver dam
and the silken pups
that frolic and play.

Your chart will note
the waters decrease.

It's all there for wise
eyes that care to see.
Black bear, deer and
sly fox without number.

My tongue will only
warn the wild ones.

RIGHTEOUS ANGER

Red Hot Rage.
Spilling and killing
as lightning strikes.
Torch the sky,
scorch the clouds.
Steam the rivers,
boil all the lakes.
Purify. Horrify.

Red Hot Rage.
Spit out harsh flames
between your teeth.
Cover the Earth,
melt the mountains,
unleash the tethered.
Destroy. Destroy.

Red Hot Rage.
Ashes to ashes,
trust to rust.
Expel your breath
burn and blister
shatter the bones.
Horrify. Purify.

mother's day roses
subtly blushed with pink
weep petals of grief

snow falling on spruce
boughs bend to shut out the wind
warmth is all around

yellow cactus blooms
grandly outshining the sun
moonlight dims their light

clouds clinging to sky
glued there by winter winds
awaiting springtime

FROM WHERE I SLID

here comes those rickety
earth moving machines again.
they'll soon be putting down
a layer of red dog shale.
time and again i watch while
they fill up the muddy ruts.

it makes it just that much
harder to gain access to
a place called Easy Street.
my view here in the hollow
has always been blocked
by deceit and detours.

GENETICS

Wallowing around
in the gene pool;
that's where you attract
all that death
and disease.

If you only have
a mudhole
to swim in
you're liable to
catch many things.

Almost daily
I hear them talking
about another new gene
they've identified,
and what it will affect.

It's a lot late
to save us from all
this inherited harm,
but our killers now
receive names.

I've learned the poor
don't inherit antiques,
but who knew that
genetic damage would
last throughout eternity?

BATTLE WEARY

one more time
i've fallen.
not failed,
but merely fallen.
weary from
constant struggle,
yet not ready
to signal defeat.
trying to hold out
and hold on,
not questioning
the what or why.
grasping at stray
bits of honey,
enough to sweeten
each tomorrow.
knowing that bitter
as life seems,
all that remains
is my fight.

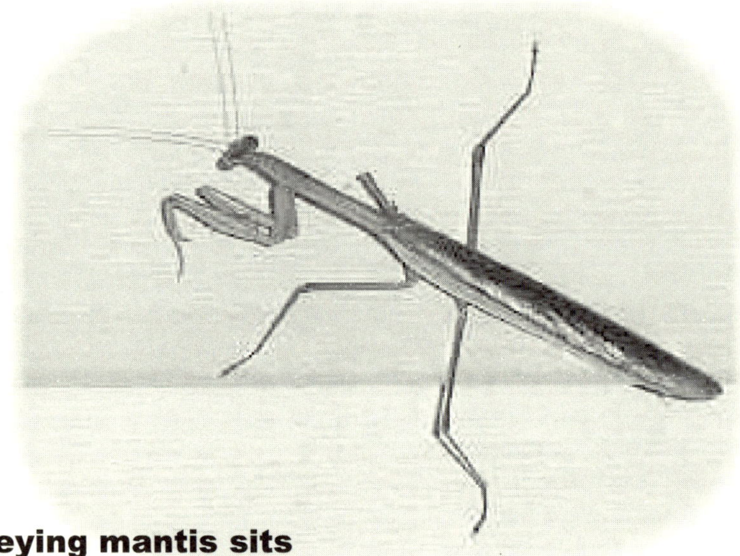

preying mantis sits
wantonly rubbing her legs
praying for a mate

vultures on the fence
awaiting the stench of death
beckons summer breeze

the local landfill
bluebird homes perch on each post
truth and beauty blur

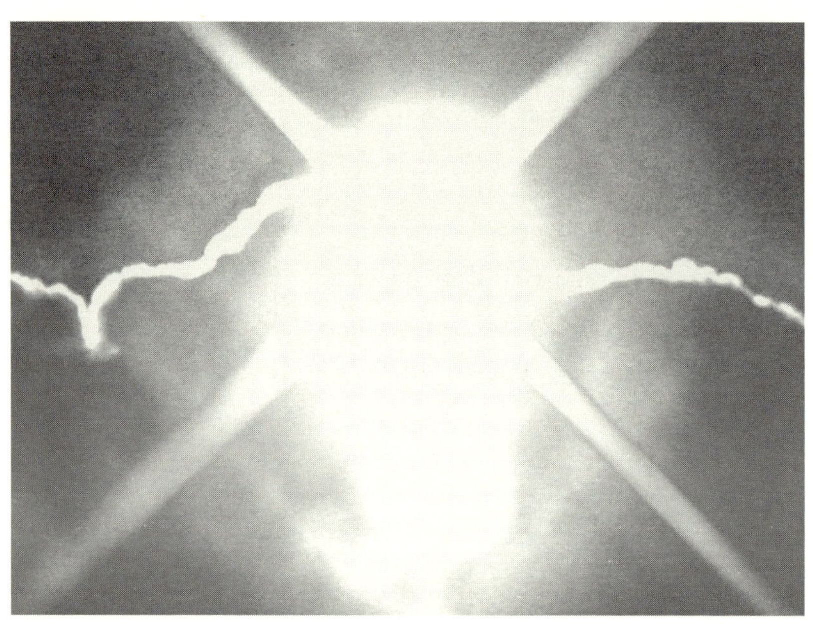

PARACHUTE PREMISE

spewed down from skies
that disdain drifters
through miles of space
in moth-chewed shroud.
fighting to stay afloat
while bargaining for
a slower descent.
knowing all the while
that i'm destined to fail.
too many weights tug
on my tangled strings
dragging me down to a
dirt-filled subsistence.
next life around
i'll opt to be a kite.
hanging from a thin line
with just enough string
to keep my feet barely
grazing the ground.

what if we had known
the true name for this yard art
witches' gazing ball

BOOK MARKED

I don't know the fools
who sat and wrote it,
but I'm sick of hearing
their list of "can'ts" quoted.

"Going by The Book,"
We're just going by
"The Book."

I need to locate
that journal of defeat.
to trash and unlearn it.

Burn it to ashes,
then grind the soot
under my boots.

Leave no page intact
until the harm
reaches a rightful end.

When change happens
you'll get treated with
respect instead of
stifled by that Book.

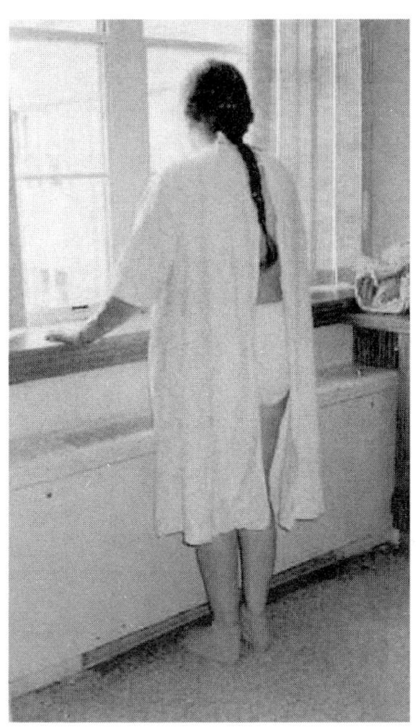

THE MEDICINE MAN

Fears are stacking
one upon another
like carvings
on a totem pole.
Each demon is
more hideous
than the last.
Shadows stalk
and taunt me
until I'm trembling
like the last leaf
on the red maple.
Can't stand the dark,
it releases bat-winged
creatures that only
day's light can banish.
Stop telling me
that the medicines
are making me paranoid.
It's my reality,
and I can't escape it.
For now, believe
in my hauntings.
In return, I'll consider
your theory of delusions,
brought on by the
pill purveyor from hell.

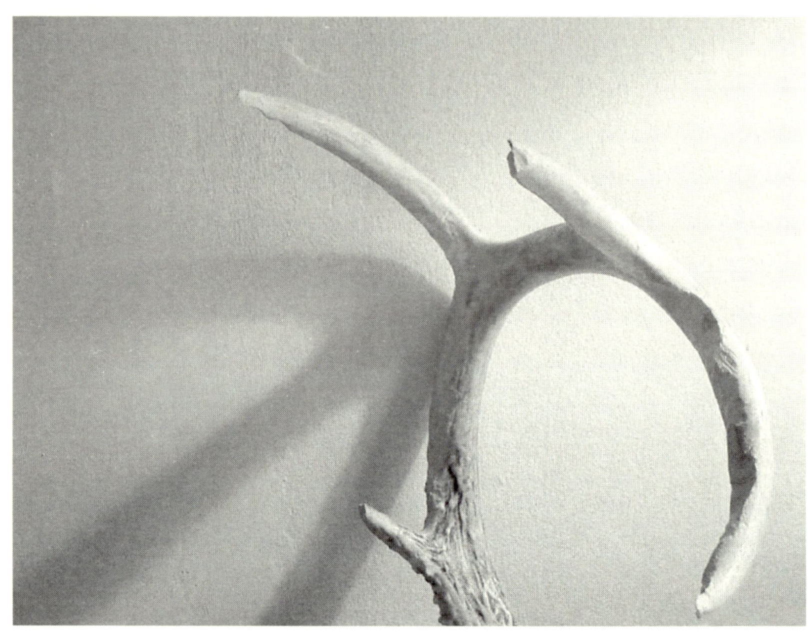

antlers in velvet
bucks rub and snort frantically
shreds cling to tree bark

knee high summer grass
mother and kid graze freely
red barn in background

squirrels at feeder
scatter weed seed that will sprout
mocking store bought

FAIRY RING FOREST

A perfect glade of green.

Just the size to
hold all of the tiny
dancing, flailing, feet.

Mushrooms circled about.

Beauty thrives
in the dampness
of a moist forest

Spongy seats for all!

The wee people nod
and bow grandly
to one another.

Music fills the night.

Round and round
the revelers twirl
no time for stopping.

Daylight too soon arrives.

With it's sodden coming
a trampled spot emerges,
and dancers slip away.

the pinto pony
sensing a summer windstorm
paws the dusty earth

Your rhyming was truly perfection,
but we feel the need for correction.
It was titled "Haiku."
We assume you are new.
Enclosed please find our rejection.

About The Author

Judith K. Witherow is a poet, essayist and storyteller. A mixed blood Native American raised in Appalachian poverty, Judith moved to Maryland as a young woman. It was too late to escape the ill effects of environmental poisoning and subsequent autoimmune disease caused by abuses of coal mining companies. She has never forgotten the harsh times of her rural youth, but she also remembers the natural ways of survival in the mountains and the overwhelming beauty of the land, the trees, the animals.

A political activist recognized primarily for her widely published essays about her experiences with disability, gender, sexual orientation, race and class, Judith also has been writing and publishing poetry for over thirty years. *All Things Wild* is a partial collection of poetry celebrating her love for all things wild and natural. It also chronicles her ongoing struggle in the rawest terms.

Judith was the winner of the first annual Audre Lorde Memorial Prose Contest for Non-fiction, April 1994.

Judith K. Witherow is online at www.jkwitherow.com.